ESCAPE!

THE EMPTY SCIENCE LAB

SOLVE YOUR WAY OUT!

Use your SCIENCE skills to ESCAPE!

Kevin Wood

Gareth Stevens
PUBLISHING

Please visit our website, www.garethstevens.com. For a free color catalog of all our high-quality books, call toll free 1-800-542-2595 or fax 1-877-542-2596.

Cataloging-in-Publication Data

Names: Wood, Kevin.
Title: The empty science lab: solve your way out! / Kevin Wood.
Description: New York : Gareth Stevens, 2023. | Series: Escape!
Identifiers: ISBN 9781538277218 (pbk.) | ISBN 9781538277232 (library bound) | ISBN 9781538277225 (6 pack) | ISBN 9781538277249 (ebook)
Subjects: LCSH: Puzzles--Juvenile literature. | Problem solving--Juvenile literature. | Logic puzzles--Juvenile literature. | Science--Juvenile literature.
Classification: LCC GV1493.W663 2023 | DDC 793.73--dc23

29 East 21st street
New York, NY 10010

Produced for Gareth Stevens Publishing by Alix Wood Books
Designed and Illustrated by Alix Wood
Editor: Eloise Macgregor

Printed in the United States of America

CPSIA compliance information: Batch # CSGS23 For further information contact Gareth Stevens, New York, New York at 1-800-542-2595.

It's your turn to help Mr. Hendricks set up the science lab. When you get to his class, the room is empty. Mr. Hendricks' classes are fun, but he always seems a little distracted. The locked laboratory doors behind Mr. Hendricks' desk fascinate you. You have never seen anyone go in, or out, all year!

Today, you can see a crack of light shining between the doors. Maybe Mr. Hendricks is back there? You look around. There is no one about. You pull on one door. It opens! As you walk through, the doors swing closed. You hear them lock behind you.

ACCESS
DENIED!

On the wall by the door, you notice some chalk scribbles. It looks like Mr. Hendricks' handwriting. Hopefully it will tell you how to unlock the door!

WARNING: If you have entered this part of the building, you will not be able to leave. The keys you need to unlock this door are too well hidden. Wait here for me. When I return, I'll let you out–once I have finished telling you off!

HOW TO ESCAPE!

Use your science knowledge to puzzle your way out of the deserted lab. Solve puzzles to get the codes you need to open a series of locked boxes. Each box contains one shaped key. You need all the shapes to open the door and escape. All the information you need to solve the puzzles can be found in this book. Clues to puzzles may be on any page, so read the whole book first.

Get stuck? Answers and hints are hidden at the back of this book.

THE CHEMISTRY LAB

You'd rather escape than be told off! Maybe you can find the hidden keys? As you enter the brightly lit chemistry lab, the smell of gas and chemicals is overpowering. Tanks of gas and jars of elements line the walls. A safe with a number pad is embedded in one wall. All you need now is a four-digit code! Surely there must be a clue somewhere?

Calcium
Ca
thium
Li
Sodium
Na
ction
6 7 8 9
Newton's Second Law
A force applied to an object at rest causes it to accelerate in the direction of the force.
Water
$H_2 + O \rightarrow H_2O$
Remember — order more helium, carbon, oxygen, and lithium
Hydrogen
H
Helium
He
Oxygen
O
Nitrogen
N
Boron
Bo
Silicon
Si

THE DESK

It looks as if Mr. Hendricks was cooking up some experiments here. Could there be a key in that locked box? If only you knew the code!

7 8 9 10 11 12 13 14
precipitation
1 2 3 4 5 6 7 8 9
Search the whole book for clues!

THE BATHROOM

Oddly, both sinks in the bathroom are full of water. Has there been some kind of experiment going on here? A code panel in the cubicle may hold a key to help your escape. Better start searching for clues!

Sink?

THE ANATOMY ROOM

Your heart skips a beat when you first see the skeleton in the anatomy lab! The skeleton in your science classroom is called "George" and Mr. Hendricks said it isn't scary. It is useful for teaching you all about bones. Some strange labels are tied onto some of the bones of this skeleton.

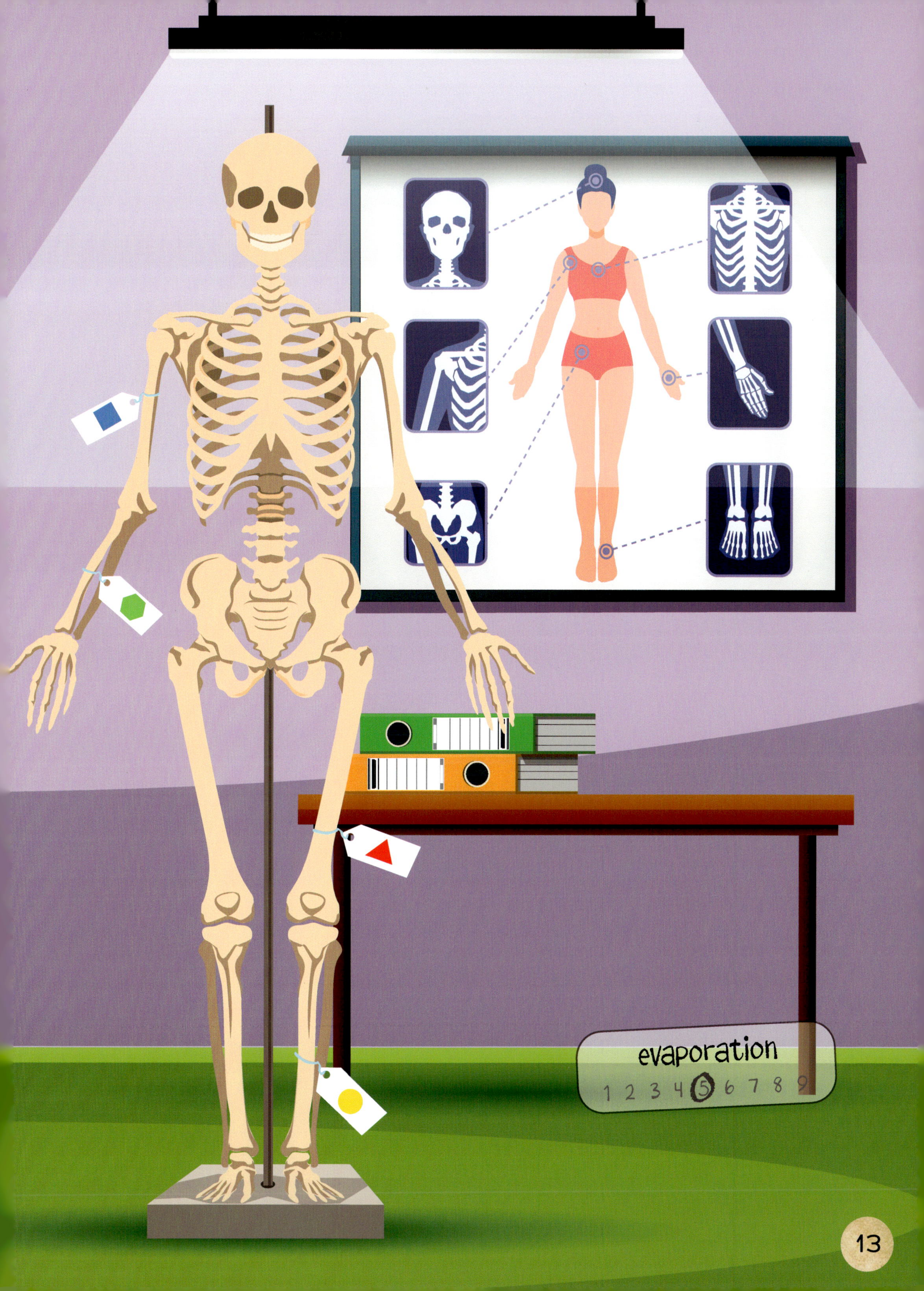

evaporation
1 2 3 4 5 6 7 8 9

THE TABLE

Back in the corridor on a table is a pile of students' notebooks, waiting to be marked. Also on the table is a scribbled note you can't read and some tiles from a game.

Maggie Newton
Science
Mr. Hendricks' Class
I ♥ Science

BIOLOGY
The Human Skeleton

Thursday March 22

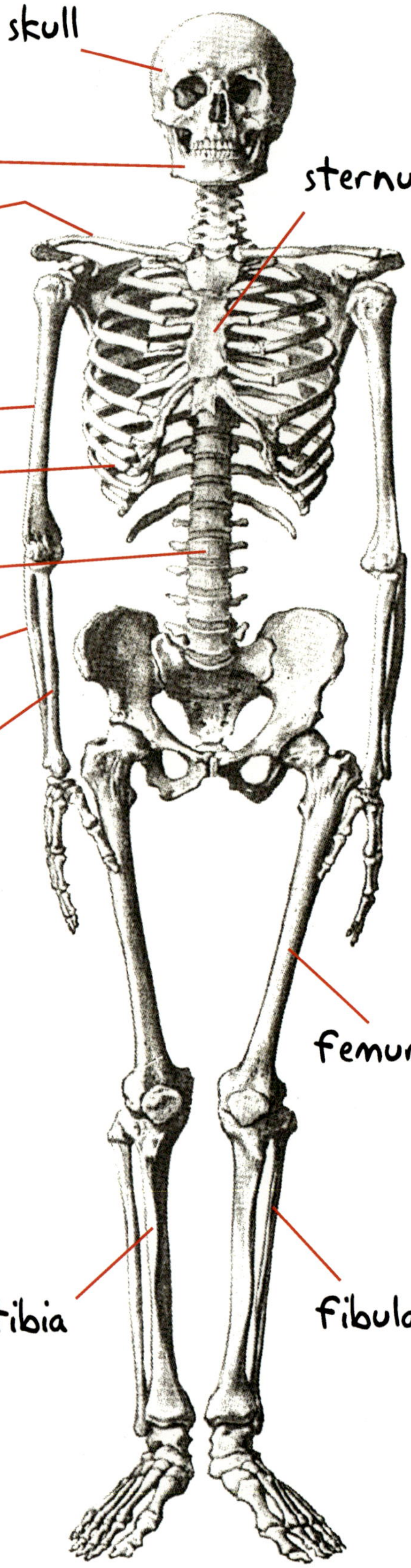

We measured George the Skeleton's bones. The six longest bones were:

	Name (common name)	Length
1	femur (thighbone)	17.8 in
2	tibia (shinbone)	16.7 in
3	fibula (lower leg)	15.9 in
4	humerus (upper arm)	14.7 in
5	ulna (inner lower arm)	11.4 in
6	radius (outer lower arm)	10.1 in

BIOLOGY

Classification of Animals

Friday March 23

Vertebrates (animals with backbones) are divided into five classes.

1. Mammals drink milk when they are babies and have hair on their body. People, dogs, and lions are mammals.

2. Birds have feathers and hatch out of hard-shelled eggs. An ostrich is a bird even though it can't fly.

3. Fish live in water and have gills, scales, and fins.

4. Reptiles have scaly skin, are cold-blooded, and are born on land. Snakes, lizards, crocodiles, and tortoises are all reptiles.

5. Amphibians are born in water, and they breathe through gills. As they grow, they develop lungs and can live on land. Frogs, newts, and toads are amphibians.

Animals without a backbone are called invertebrates. Spiders, crabs, and snails are invertebrates.

Types of Diet: Herbivores, Carnivores, and Omnivores

Herbivores only eat plants. Rabbits and iguanas are herbivores.

Carnivores only eat meat. Snakes and owls are carnivores. Frogs are carnivores, but when they are tadpoles, they are herbivores.

Omnivores eat both plants and meat. Chickens, rats, and pigs are omnivores.

BIOLOGY

Monday March 26

Plants

Fruits protect the seeds.

Leaves capture sunlight and use it to turn carbon dioxide gas into plant food and oxygen.

Seeds can develop into another plant.

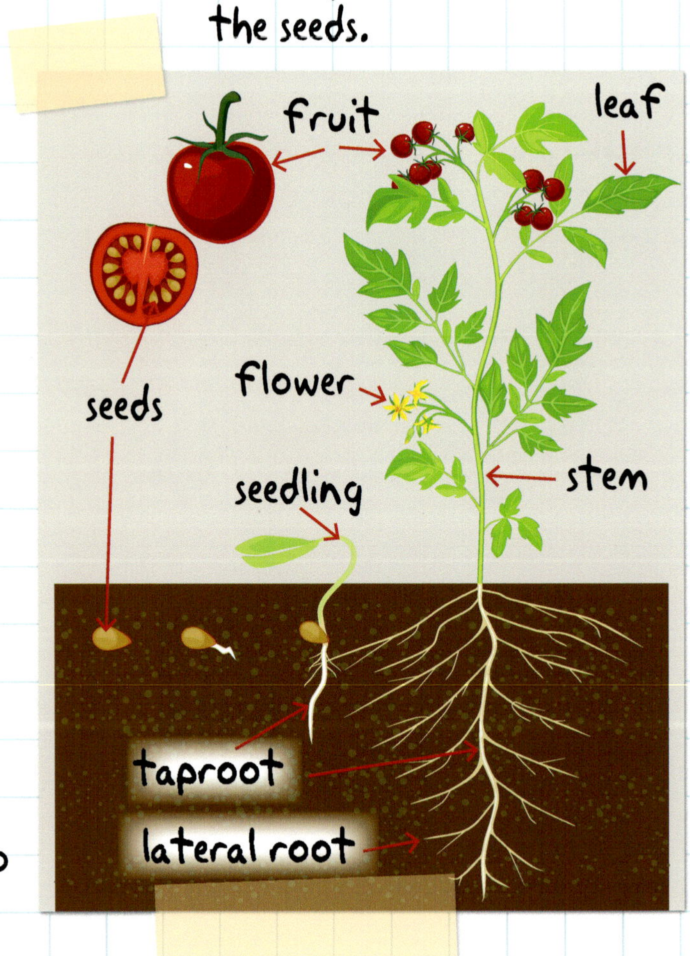

Flowers attract insects such as butterflies and bees to the plant to pollinate them so the plant can produce seeds.

The stem transports nutrients and minerals up to the rest of the plant.

Roots pull water and minerals into the plant, and anchor it to the ground.

CHEMISTRY

Tuesday March 27

The pH Scale

The pH scale helps us measure how alkaline or acidic a solution is. 0 is the most acidic. 14 is the most alkaline. Water is neutral, with a pH of 7. We can test solutions by adding a drop of pH indicator. The indicator colors the liquid to match one of the colors in this table. We can also use litmus paper. Blue litmus paper turns red in an acid. Red litmus paper turns blue in an alkali.

PHYSICS

Wednesday March 28

Sir Isaac Newton's Laws of Motion.

Third Law - For every action, there is an equal and opposite reaction.

When you push against something, the "something" pushes back just as hard. If you push a car, the car pushes back against you with the same amount of force.

The Periodic Table of Elements

The periodic table is a chart of all known chemical elements. Elements in the table are placed in order of their atomic number. For example, hydrogen, with the symbol H, has an atomic number of 1.

1 H																	2 He
3 Li	4 Be											5 B	6 C	7 N	8 O	9 F	10 Ne
11 Na	12 Mg											13 Al	14 Si	15 P	16 S	17 Cl	18 Ar
19 K	20 Ca	21 Sc	22 Ti	23 V	24 Cr	25 Mn	26 Fe	27 Co	28 Ni	29 Cu	30 Zn	31 Ga	32 Ge	33 As	34 Se	35 Br	36 Kr
37 Rb	38 Sr	39 Y	40 Zr	41 Nb	42 Mo	43 Tc	44 Ru	45 Rh	46 Pd	47 Ag	48 Cd	49 In	50 Sn	51 Sb	52 Te	53 I	54 Xe
55 Cs	56 Ba	57 La*	72 Hf	73 Ta	74 W	75 Re	76 Os	77 Ir	78 Pt	79 Au	80 Hg	81 Tl	82 Pb	83 Bi	84 Po	85 At	86 Rn
87 Fr	88 Ra	89 Ac**	104 Rf	105 Db	106 Sg	107 Bh	108 Hs	109 Mt	110 Ds	111 Rg	112 Cn	113 Nh	114 Fl	115 Mc	116 Lv	117 Ts	118 Og

Homework - Learn the symbols along the top two rows by Friday!

*	58 Ce	59 Pr	60 Nd	61 Pm	62 Sm	63 Eu	64 Gd	65 Tb	66 Dy	67 Ho	68 Er	69 Tm	70 Yb	71 Lu
**	90 Th	91 Pa	92 U	93 Np	94 Pu	95 Am	96 Cm	97 Bk	98 Cf	99 Es	100 Fm	101 Md	102 No	103 Lr

THE CUPBOARD

Beside the desk is a large cupboard. The shelves are packed full of toys. A small note is taped onto a large blue space hopper. It reads: "To float is the key to escaping your troubles." How deep!

THE BOTANY CENTER

Mr. Hendricks loved teaching about plants. If only I could remember everything he taught us, it might get me out of here. Perhaps we need to enter a code into that vending machine?

Know Your Plants
A
B
C
D
E
F
G
H
AUTOMATIC PLANT FEED
A B C D
E F G H
AUTOMATIC

THE ANIMAL BARN

As the door to the barn creaks open, all the birds and animals look at you hopefully. It doesn't look as if they have been fed yet. I think some may have escaped through that tiny crack in the door. Perhaps you should feed them? But who eats what? The food storage bin is padlocked, with a note taped on it.

Animal Count
Reptiles?
Will eat meat?
Invertebrates?

THE CORRIDOR

Sunlight streams through the large window along the corridor. Such a beautiful view of the waterfall! A half-finished diagram has been drawn on a glass screen. A locked filing cabinet stands in one corner. Perhaps one of the keys is inside it? But what could the code be?

States of Matter
gas
liquid
solid
HOT
COLD
12
9
3
6

THE PLANETARIUM

It is beginning to get dark. You stumble in the gloomy passageway and lean on a button. A pair of double doors slowly start to slide open. An unlit room with huge windows lies beyond. Your eyes gradually adjust to the moonlight. You make out a line of planets hung on wire from the ceiling. Charts and bookshelves full of facts about astronomy cover the walls. A telescope points out to the night sky. There is a safe on one wall.

Saturn
Uranus
Neptune
transpiration
1 2 3 4 5 6 7 8 9

THE KITCHEN

The kitchen is in a bit of a state. If there is a key safe in this room, it's not obvious where it is, or what the code could be, for that matter. A botany test paper sits on a recipe book stand.

Botany Center Lab Staff Test

Which part of a plant anchors it to the ground?
A) the leaves B) the seeds C) the roots D) the flower

Look at the "Know Your Plants" poster. Which letter label is pointing to the lateral root?
A, B, C, D, E, F, G, or H?

Which part of a plant changes carbon dioxide gas into nutrients?
A) the leaves B) the seeds C) the roots D) the flower

What part of a plant attracts insects to help the plant reproduce?
A) the leaves B) the seeds C) the roots D) the flower

Did you escape the science lab?
Check your answers on page 32.

HINTS

The Chemistry Lab
1. Could all those bottles and jars hold the clue?
2. The notebook may be able to help.
3. Which chemicals, in what order? Maybe you can find a chalky clue?

The Desk
1. What are those dishes and strips of paper for?
2. Looks like some kind of kitchen chemistry experiment!
3. The notebook may help with the recipe for success.

The Bathroom
1. Colors, not numbers? Interesting.
2. Are there any more ducks anywhere?
3. How many on the shelf don't get that sinking feeling?

The Anatomy Room
1. The labels seem to match the cabinet buttons.
2. Could there be some help in the notebook?
3. Not the length, but the position?

The Table
1. Give this problem a little reflection.
2. Sir Isaac may be able to help.
3. The tiles hold the answer.

The Botany Center
1. Do you need me to draw you a picture?
2. Revise the botany notes . . .
3. . . . and then answer the questions.

The Animal Barn
1. The notebook may help you.
2. Some of those animals have escaped; get searching.
3. Three questions, four numbers? Is one two digits?

The Corridor
1. Does that view look familiar?
2. Maybe those empty colored outlines need filling?
3. Right word = right number.

The Planetarium
1. Search everywhere for other information about the planets.
2. Answering questions may give you the numbers you need.
3. That bright star may not be where you expect.

The Kitchen
1. What could help you cook up the answer?
2. One of Mr. Hendricks' posters may hold the key.
3. Order them left to right from the kitchen.

ANSWERS

A mirror will help you read these answers.

6-7: 2683 [the atomic numbers for helium, carbon, oxygen, and lithium]

8-9: 6982 [the pH numbers of milk, baking soda, egg, and lemon juice from the recipe]

10-11: 4615 [the number of things that would float on each colored shelf]

12-13: 1462 [the order number for the length of each bone]

14-15: 1113111 [the numbers on the tiles that spell "reaction"]

22-23: CGAD [the answers to the quiz on page 30]

24-25: 5 15 2 [answers to the list on the feed bin; how many animals pictured in the book are reptiles, eat meat, and are invertebrates]

26-27: 2591 [the numbers on the correct words from the water cycle diagram, with the corresponding border color]

28-29: 869 [the answers to the blackboard planet questions on page 26]

30-31: Spiral, circle, square [the shapes of the steam, water, and ice in the kitchen and on the poster]